Fireflies

ABDO Publishing Company

Big Buddy BOOKS
Insects

Julie Murray

VISIT US AT
www.abdopublishing.com

Published by ABDO Publishing Company, 8000 West 78th Street, Edina, Minnesota 55439.

Copyright © 2011 by Abdo Consulting Group, Inc. International copyrights reserved in all countries. No part of this book may be reproduced in any form without written permission from the publisher. Big Buddy Books™ is a trademark and logo of ABDO Publishing Company.

Printed in the United States of America, North Mankato, Minnesota.
042010
092010

 PRINTED ON RECYCLED PAPER

Coordinating Series Editor: Rochelle Baltzer
Editor: Sarah Tieck
Contributing Editors: Heidi M.D. Elston, Megan M. Gunderson, BreAnn Rumsch, Marcia Zappa
Graphic Design: Maria Hosley
Cover Photograph: *Minden Pictures*: ©Atsuo Fujimaru/Nature Productions.
Interior Photographs/Illustrations: *AnimalsAnimals-Earth Scenes*: ©LLOYD, JAMES (p. 30); *Getty Images*: Isao Kuroda (p. 15), Steven Puetzer (p. 13), Paul A. Zahl/National Geographic (pp. 11, 13, 27); *iStockphoto*: ©iStockphoto.com/ABDESIGN (pp. 5, 17), ©iStockphoto.com/Terryfic3D (pp. 5, 23); *Minden Pictures*: Satoshi Kuribayashi/Nature Production (p. 17); *Peter Arnold, Inc.*: ©Biosphoto/Cavignaux Bruno (p. 19), Hans Pfletschinger (p. 9), Jeffrey L. Rotman (p. 30); *Photo Researchers, Inc.*: Darwin Dale (p. 7), Eye of Science (p. 11), Noah Poritz (p. 25), Gregory K. Scott (p. 21); *Shutterstock*: Cathy Keifer (pp. 5, 12), Alexey Stipp (pp. 5, 29).

Library of Congress Cataloging-in-Publication Data

Murray, Julie, 1969-
  Fireflies / Julie Murray.
    p. cm. -- (Insects)
  ISBN 978-1-61613-485-3
  1. Fireflies--Juvenile literature. I. Title. II. Series: Murray, Julie, 1969- Insects.
  QL596.L28M87 2011
  595.76'44--dc22
                        2010002524

Contents

Insect World

    Millions of insects live throughout the world. They are found on the ground, in the air, and in the water. Some have existed since before there were dinosaurs!

    Fireflies are one type of insect. Most live in watery areas including swamps, rivers, and marshes. You may even see fireflies in your backyard!

Bug Bite!

Fireflies are a type of beetle.

A firefly's body is brown or black. It has red, orange, or yellow markings.

A Firefly's Body

Most fireflies are less than one inch (3 cm) long. Like all insects, they have three main body parts. These are the head, the **thorax**, and the **abdomen**.

A firefly's head has strong **jaws** and two large eyes. Its two antennae help the firefly touch and smell.

Six legs connect to the thorax. Many fireflies have two pairs of wings on the thorax, too. Important **organs** are inside the abdomen.

Bug Bite!

A firefly breathes through tiny holes on its abdomen.

Antennae

Head

Eyes

Thorax

Legs

Abdomen

Wings

Life in the Air

When people think of fireflies, they picture flying lights. Adult fireflies have outer wings called elytra (EH-luh-truh). These **protect** the softer inner wings. To fly, fireflies open their elytra and flap their inner wings.

Fireflies mostly fly at night. During the day, many rest in bushes, grasses, and trees. Their legs bend in many places. This helps them grab hold of surfaces and climb.

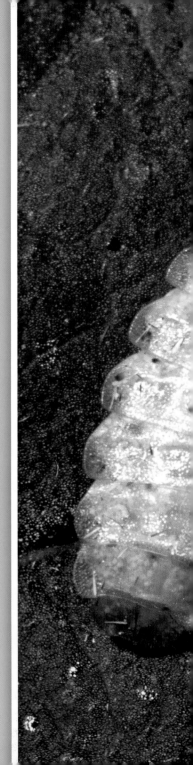

Some types of female (*left*) fireflies have no wings. They are often called glowworms.

Fireflies have large eyes. Each eye has hundreds of tiny lenses. So, fireflies don't see one clear image like people do. Each lens sees a different part of the picture.

Still, fireflies see light and movement very well. This helps them as they fly through the air.

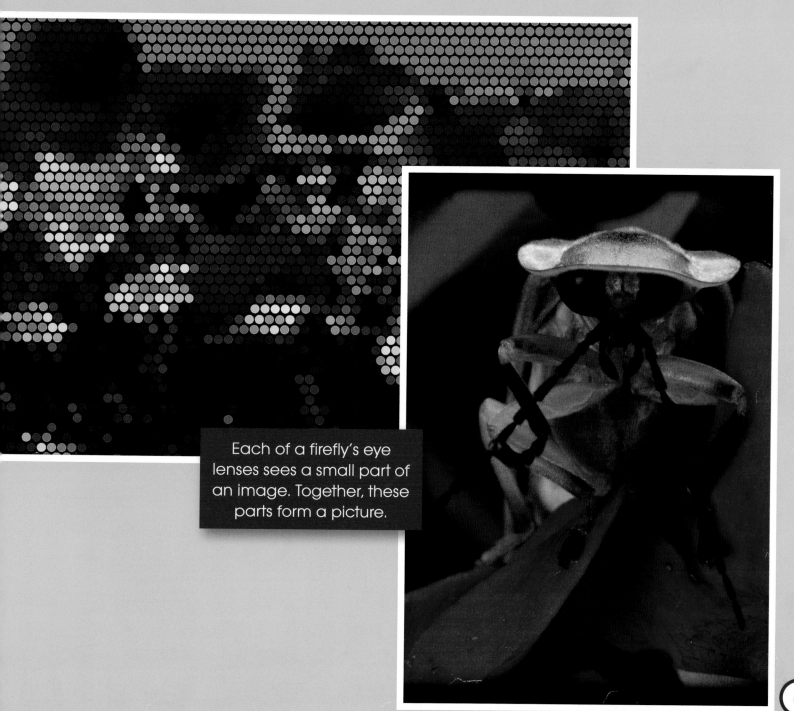

Each of a firefly's eye lenses sees a small part of an image. Together, these parts form a picture.

Living Lights

Living things that make light are called bioluminescent (beye-oh-loo-muh-NEH-suhnt).

Bug Bite!

In South America, some people wear bags of fireflies around their wrists and ankles for light.

Some people collect fireflies in jars.

Fireflies can glow enough to provide light for reading.

Fireflies are famous for lighting up. Their bodies produce **chemicals** called luciferin and luciferase. When these chemicals mix with oxygen, they give off light.

This mixing happens in an **organ** called the lantern. A firefly's lantern is on the underside of its **abdomen**. The light created there is heatless. So, the lantern feels cool when touched.

Flash Patterns

There are more than 1,000 kinds of fireflies. Most firefly types have their own pattern of light flashes.

These patterns help fireflies find each other to **mate**. Males flash from the sky as they fly. Females flash back from a plant or the ground. Then, the males land to mate.

Bug Bite! Temperatures affect fireflies. When it is cold, they flash more slowly.

Bug Bite!

Not all adult fireflies glow!

When many fireflies glow at once, their light shows from far away.

Life Begins

The firefly life cycle has four stages. These are egg, larva, pupa, and adult.

Like other insects, all fireflies begin life as eggs. After **mating**, the female firefly lays her eggs in a **damp** place. Most female fireflies lay their eggs on or in soil.

Bug Bite!

In some parts of the United States, fireflies are called lightning bugs.

Life Cycle of a Firefly

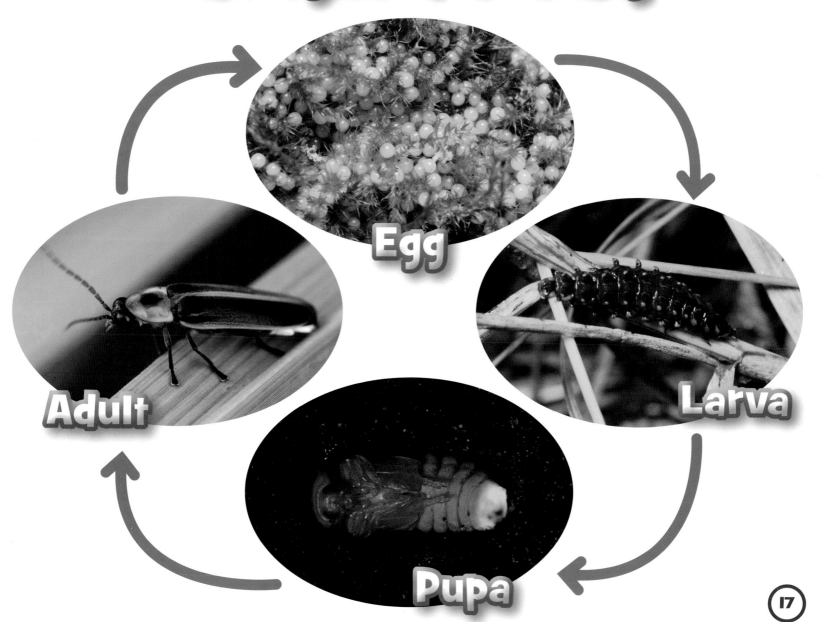

Egg

Larva

Pupa

Adult

Growing Up

Inside each egg, a firefly larva grows. Then, the larva **hatches** from its egg.

Firefly larvae spend most of their time eating. They squirt poison into their **prey**. This turns it to liquid. Then, the larvae suck up their dinner!

Firefly larvae eat snails, small insects, and worms.

Firefly larvae have many enemies. Birds, fish, toads, and frogs eat them. Larvae may taste bad or be poisonous to some predators. This helps **protect** them. Larvae also hide from enemies in **damp**, dark places. They often find spots under rotting logs and leaf piles.

Bug Bite!

Some larvae squirt poison at predators who try to eat them.

Firefly larvae are also called glowworms. Their glow warns predators that they may be poisonous or taste bad.

Becoming a Firefly

Most fireflies are larvae for one to two years. Many firefly larvae rest during cold winter months.

In spring, larvae enter the pupa stage. As pupae, they rest without eating. Wings form during this stage. Soon, the pupa's skin splits open. Then, an adult firefly crawls out.

During the day, it is hard to see a firefly's lantern hidden beneath its body.

Adult Fireflies

Most adult fireflies spend their days resting under grasses and leaves. They are usually active at night.

Adult fireflies generally live between 5 and 30 days. An adult's most important job is to **mate**. This keeps the firefly population growing.

Fireflies don't live in just one spot. They move around within an area.

Bug Bite!

Most adult fireflies don't eat often. They live off of food they ate as larvae. But sometimes, they eat nectar.

Danger Zone

Adult fireflies face many predators. These include birds, frogs, and spiders.

Yet adults have certain features to **protect** them. Like larvae, they taste bitter or are poisonous to many predators. A firefly's light is a warning of this.

Bug Bite!

Some frogs eat so many fireflies that they glow!

Spiderwebs are sticky traps. If a firefly gets caught in one, it is hard to get free.

Special Insects

Fireflies help keep the natural world in balance. They serve as food for many animals. Fireflies are useful to people, too. In some parts of the world, people use them for light. And, scientists use luciferin and luciferase for medical purposes. Fireflies are important to life on Earth.

Different types of fireflies have different color lights. Some glow a yellow-green color, while others glow green or amber.

Bug-O-Rama

Do any other animals glow?

Many types of insects, sea animals, and even germs glow. Most of these animals, such as jellyfish (*right*), live deep in the ocean. Their world is dark all the time.

Are fireflies smart?

Yes! Some types of female fireflies can copy the flash pattern of other kinds of fireflies. To draw in males, a female flashes these patterns. When a male lands near her, she kills it and eats it for dinner!

Can fireflies flash together?

Actually, yes. Males of some types of fireflies meet in one spot. Then, thousands of them flash at the same time. Scientists aren't sure why they do this. It may help females notice them. Or, it may be a way for males to compete.

Important Words

abdomen (AB-duh-muhn) the back part of an insect's body.

chemical (KEH-mih-kuhl) a substance that can cause reactions and changes.

damp slightly wet.

hatch to be born from an egg.

jaws a mouthpart that allows for holding, crushing, and chewing.

mate to join as a couple in order to reproduce, or have babies.

organ a body part that does a special job. The heart and the lungs are organs.

prey an animal hunted or killed by a predator for food.

protect (pruh-TEHKT) to guard against harm or danger.

thorax the middle part of an insect's body.

Web Sites

To learn more about fireflies, visit ABDO Publishing Company online. Web sites about fireflies are featured on our Book Links page. These links are routinely monitored and updated to provide the most current information available.

www.abdopublishing.com

Index